Cori spezzati

VOLUME II

Cori spezzati deals with polychoral church music from its beginnings in the first few decades of the sixteenth century to its climax in the work of Giovanni Gabrieli and Heinrich Schütz. In polychoral music the singers, sometimes with instrumentalists also, were split into two (or more) groups which often engaged in lively dialogue and joined in majestic tutti climaxes. The first volume draws on contemporary descriptions of the idiom, especially from the writings of Vicentino and Zarlino, but concentrates in the main on musical analysis, showing how antiphonal chanting (such as that of the psalms), dialogue and canon influenced the phenomenon. Polychoral music often has been considered synonymous not only with Venetian music but with impressive pomp. Anthony Carver's study shows that it was cultivated by many composers outside Venice – in Rome, all over Northern Italy, in Catholic and Protestant areas of Germany, in Spain and the New World – and that it was as capable of quiet devotion or mannerist expressionism as of outgoing pomp. Perhaps most important, music by several major composers about which there is still surprisingly little in the literature is treated in depth: the Gabrielis, Lasso, Palestrina, Victoria, and several German masters. Volume I is illustrated with many musical examples.

This companion volume offers an anthology of seventeen complete pieces, most of which are analysed in the text of volume I.

Cori spezzati

VOLUME II
AN ANTHOLOGY OF
SACRED POLYCHORAL MUSIC

EDITED BY
ANTHONY F. CARVER

Senior Lecturer in Music
The Queen's University of Belfast

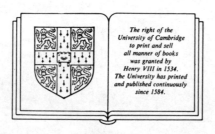

The right of the
University of Cambridge
to print and sell
all manner of books
was granted by
Henry VIII in 1534.
The University has printed
and published continuously
since 1584.

CAMBRIDGE UNIVERSITY PRESS

Cambridge
New York   New Rochelle   Melbourne   Sydney

Published by the Press Syndicate of the University of Cambridge
The Pitt Building, Trumpington Street, Cambridge CB2 1RP
32 East 57th Street, New York, NY 10022, USA
10 Stamford Road, Oakleigh, Melbourne 3166, Australia

First published 1988

Printed in Great Britain at
the University Press, Cambridge

British Library cataloguing in publication data
Cori spezzati.
Vol. 2: An anthology of sacred polychoral
music.
1. Cori spezzati – History and criticism
I. Carver, Anthony F.
783.4   ML1554

Library of Congress cataloguing in publication data
An anthology of sacred polychoral music.
(Cori spezzati; v. II)
Contents: Ps. 133: Ecce nunc benedicite/Francesco
Santacroce – Nostra ut pura/Costanzo Festa – Regina
Caeli/Jean Rousée – [etc.]
1. Choruses, Sacred. 2. Motets. 3. Masses,
Unaccompanied – Excerpts. I. Carver, Anthony F.
II. Series.
M1.C79   1988   vol. II   [M1999]   87-753501

ISBN 0 521 30398 2 Volume I
ISBN 0 521 30399 0 Volume II
ISBN 0 521 36172 9 the set

CONTENTS

ACKNOWLEDGMENTS

My grateful thanks are due to the following for allowing me to prepare editions from manuscript or printed material in their possession: Bayerische Staatsbibliothek, Munich (no. 9); Biblioteca Apostolica Vaticana, Rome (no. 2); Biblioteca Capitolare, Treviso (no. 1); Österreichische Nationalbibliothek, Vienna (nos. 3 & 7); to the following for permission to use copyright material: Hänssler-Verlag, D-7303 Neuhausen–Stuttgart (no. 4, from D. Phinot, *Opera omnia*, vol. 4, ed. J. Höfler, © Copyright 1982 by American Institute of Musicology; no. 15, from G. Gabrieli, *Opera omnia*, vol. 1, ed. D. Arnold, © Copyright 1956 by Armen Carapetyan; no. 16, from G. Gabrieli, *Opera omnia*, vol. 3, ed. D. Arnold, © Copyright 1962 by Armen Carapetyan); Bärenreiter-Verlag, D-3500 Kassel (no. 10b, from O. di Lasso, *Sämtliche Werke, neue Reihe*, vol. 10, ed. S. Hermelink, © Copyright 1970 by Bärenreiter-Verlag); Istituto Italiano per la Storia della Musica (no. 11, from G. P. da Palestrina, *Le opere complete*, vol. 33, ed. L. Bianchi, © Copyright 1981 by Istituto Italiano per la Storia della Musica); VEB Deutscher Verlag für Musik (no. 17, from S. Scheidt, *Werke*, vol. 4, ed. G. Harms & C. Mahrenholz, © Copyright 1933 by VEB Deutscher Verlag für Musik); and to Dr Brian Scott for his help with some of the translations.

I

PS. 133 ECCE NUNC BENEDICITE

Francesco Santacroce

1. Ec - ce nunc be - ne - di - ci - te Do - mi - num,

CANTUS

ALTUS

TENOR

BASSUS

CANTUS SECUNDUS

ALTUS SECUNDUS

TENOR SECUNDUS

BASSUS SECUNDUS

2
INVIOLATA, INTEGRA
ET CASTA ES

Secunda pars

Costanzo Festa

3
REGINA CAELI

Jean Rousée

4
SANCTA TRINITAS

Dominique Phinot

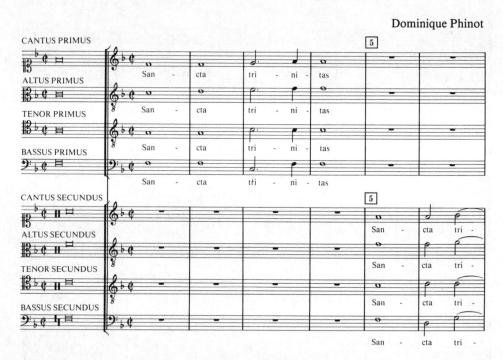

5
QUEM VIDISTIS, PASTORES?

Francisco Bonardo

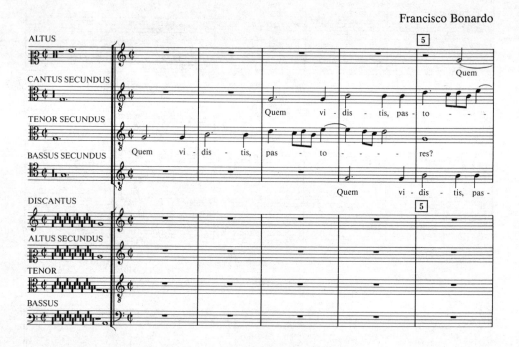

6
PS. 99 JUBILATE DEO

Alexander Utendal

7
MASS À 24: AGNUS DEI

Annibale Padovano

49

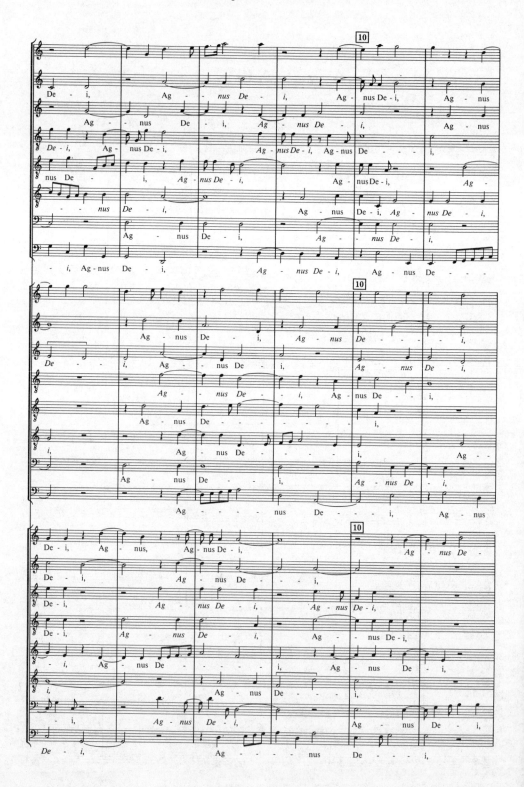

8
PS. 125 IN CONVERTENDO DOMINUS

Orlando di Lasso

56

9
EPITAPHIUM DIVI BERNARDI:
Mira loquor

Orlando di Lasso

10(a)
OSCULETUR ME OSCULO

Orlando di Lasso

75

10(b)
MISSA SUPER OSCULETUR ME: KYRIE

Orlando di Lasso

II
VIDENTES STELLAM MAGI

Giovanni Pierluigi da Palestrina

12
MAGNIFICAT PRIMI TONI

Tomás Luis de Victoria

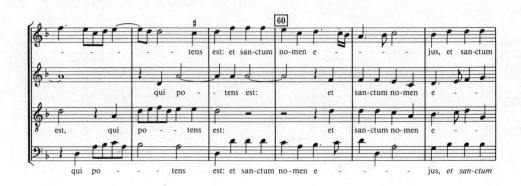

7. De-po-su- it po-ten - tes de   se   de,   et ex - al - ta - vit hu - mi - les.

7. De-po-su- it po-ten - tes   de se   de,   et ex - al - ta - vit hu - mi - les.

7. De-po-su- it po-ten - tes   de   se - - - de,   et ex - al - ta - vit hu - mi - les.

7. De-po-su- it po-ten - tes   de   se - - - de,   et ex - al - ta - vit hu - mi - les.

8. E - su - ri - en - - - tes   im - ple - vit   bo - - - nis: et di - vi-tes di-

8. E - su - ri - en - - - tes   im - ple - vit   bo - - - nis: et di - vi-tes di-

8. E - su - ri - en - - - tes   im - ple - vit bo - - - nis: et di - vi-tes di-

8. E - su - ri - en - - - tes   im - ple - vit bo - - - nis: et di - vi-tes di-

im - ple - vit bo - - - - nis: et

im - ple - vit bo - - - nis: et

im - ple - vit bo - nis, im - ple - vit bo - nis: et

im - ple - vit   bo - - - nis: et

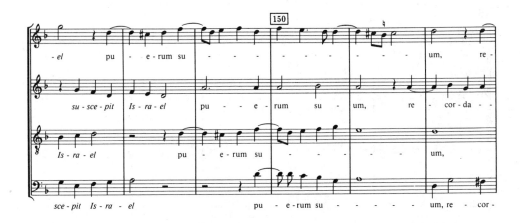

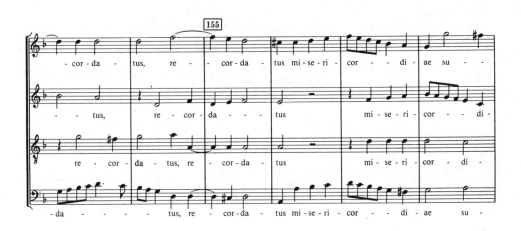

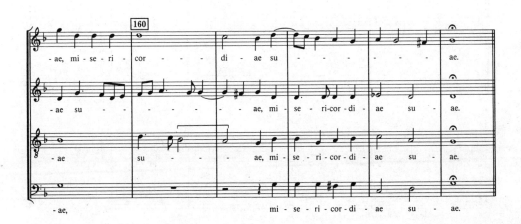

13
QUEM VIDISTIS, PASTORES?

Andrea Gabrieli

14
BENEDICAM DOMINUM

Andrea Gabrieli

15
O DOMINE JESU CHRISTE

Giovanni Gabrieli

16
HODIE COMPLETI SUNT

Giovanni Gabrieli

17
NU KOMM DER HEYDEN HEYLAND

Samuel Scheidt

EDITORIAL COMMENTARY

Sources

Details of sources are given below. In pieces taken from modern editions, some alterations have been made to produce, as far as possible, typographical and editorial uniformity within this anthology. In the commentary, citations are abbreviated as follows: bar number, voice-part, beat of the bar, reading in the source. Thus '43Q3 precautionary ×' indicates a × sign in the source before the note in the Quintus on the third beat of bar 43. Where voice-parts are not named in the source, they are referred to by number according to their position in the score, beginning at the top.

Time signatures, note values and bar-lines

In duple time, the original signature has been retained but, with the exception of no. 16, note values have been halved. In triple time the note values have been either halved or quartered and the modern signatures of, respectively, 3/2 or 3/4 inserted. All bar-lines are editorial and have been inserted as far as possible at regular intervals. Coloration is indicated by broken brackets, ligatures by continuous brackets.

Accidentals

The music is to be read according to the modern convention that an accidental in a particular voice-part applies to the end of that bar unless contradicted. Accidentals in the source which this convention renders redundant have been omitted unless they appear to have particular significance. Accidentals which are necessary because of the bar-line convention have been inserted before the note in brackets, as have accidentals which are precautionary for any other reason. Accidentals placed above the note have been inserted editorially. Modern usage has been followed in the matter of sharp and natural signs.

Text underlay

The intention has been, where the underlay in the source is ambiguous, to provide a singable version. Text in italics is either not present in the source or indicated by repetition signs such as 'ij'. Latin spellings have been modernised.

1. Francesco Santacroce: *Ps. 133 Ecce nunc benedicite*

Source: Treviso, Biblioteca Capitolare, Ms. 24a: f. 65v; Ms. 24b: f. 61v. Incipit from Ms. 22: f. 41v. (For variants in Verona, Accademia Filarmonica, Ms. 218, see Carver 1980: 365–6.)

Comments: 17, 23: no change of time signature.

Translation:

1. Behold, now, bless the Lord, all you servants of the Lord.
2. Who stand in the house of the Lord, in the halls of the house of our God.
3. By night lift up your hands in the holy place, and bless the Lord.
4. May the Lord bless you from Sion, who has made heaven and earth.
5. Glory be to the Father, and to the Son, and to the Holy Spirit.
6. As it was in the beginning, is now, and ever shall be, world without end. Amen.

(The last psalm of Compline on feast-days)

2. Costanzo Festa: *Nostra ut pura* (*Secunda pars* of *Inviolata, integra et casta es*)

Source: Rome, Biblioteca Apostolica Vaticana, Cap. Sist. Cod. 20, f. 122v.

Comments: The manuscript is in a rather poor state of preservation, and the present transcription, made from photocopies, is conjectural at some points.

Translation:

In order that our souls and bodies might be pure,
Which now our devout hearts and lips demand,
By your sweet-sounding prayers, grant us pardon for ever.

(Sequence in honour of the Blessed Virgin, middle stanza)

3. Jean Rousée: *Regina caeli*

Source: Liber duodecimus: XVII. musicales ad virginem Christiparam salutationes habet. Paris, P. Attaingnant, 1535 (RISM 1535[(4)]): f. 5v.

Translation:

O Queen of heaven, rejoice, alleluia: for he whom you were deemed worthy to bear, alleluia: has risen, as he said, alleluia. Pray for us to God, alleluia.

(Antiphon, sung after Compline from Easter Sunday until the Friday after Pentecost)

4. Dominique Phinot: *Sancta trinitas*

Source: Dominique Phinot, *Opera omnia*, vol. 4, ed. Janez Höfler. Neuhausen–Stuttgart, American Institute of Musicology, 1982: 164.

Translation:

O Holy Trinity, one God, have mercy upon us. We call upon you, we praise you, we adore you, we glorify you, O blessed Trinity. May the name of the Lord be blessed from this time forth and for evermore.

(An invocation to the Trinity, of no fixed liturgical position)

5. Francisco Bonardo: *Quem vidistis, pastores?*

Source: Thesaurus musicus continens selectissimas octo, septem, sex, quinque et quatuor vocum Harmonias...Tomi primi. Nuremberg, J. Montanus & U. Neuber, 1564 (RISM 1564[(1)]): no. 57.

Comments: 22A2: *sic*; perhaps the d' should read g'. 26B²2: d. 89TI: ♪.

Translation:

What did you see, shepherds? Tell us, announce to us, who appeared on the earth? A birth we saw, and a chorus of angels praising the Lord, saying: Glory to God in the highest, and on earth peace to men of goodwill. Alleluia.

(Antiphon at Lauds on the Feast of the Nativity, amplified with Luke 2:14)

6. Alexander Utendal: *Ps. 99 Jubilate Deo*

Sources: Alexander Utendal, *Sacrae cantiones sex, et plurium vocum. . .liber secundus.* Nuremberg, T. Gerlach, 1573 (RISM U 121): no. 18 (all except B²); *Novi atque catholici thesauri musici. Liber secundus.* Venice, A. Gardano, 1568 (RISM 1568⁽³⁾): 223 (B²).

Comments: 13–15C²: text reads 'In conspectu' instead of 'Introite'.

Translation:

1. Shout to God all you lands: serve the Lord with gladness.
2. Come into his presence with exultation.
3. Know that the Lord himself is God: he himself has made us, and not we ourselves.
4. We are his people, and the sheep of his pasture: enter his gates testifying, his courts with a hymn: acknowledge him.
5. Praise his name: for the Lord is good, eternal is his mercy, to all generations his truth.

(A psalm from Lauds of feasts, here lacking the doxology)

7. Annibale Padovano: *Agnus Dei* (from Mass à 24)

Source: Vienna, Österreichische Nationalbibliothek, Ms. 16702 I–III, f. 240v.

Translation:

Lamb of God, who takes away the sin of the world: have mercy upon us.
Lamb of God, who takes away the sin of the world: grant us peace.

(From the Ordinary of the Mass)

8. Orlando di Lasso: *Ps. 125 In convertendo Dominus*

Source: Novi atque catholici thesauri musici. Liber quartus. Venice, A. Gardano, 1568 (RISM 1568⁽⁵⁾): 353.

Comments: 43Q3: precautionary ×. 50C3: ♩ . Bar 70: signature 3 in all parts. 83C4: ×.

Translation:

1. When the Lord turned the captivity of Sion: we became as those who are consoled.
2. Then our mouth was filled with joy: and our tongue with exultation.
3. Then they said among the peoples: the Lord has done great things for them.
4. The Lord has done great things for us: we have been made glad.
5. Turn, O Lord, our captivity, like the torrents of the Negeb.
6. Those who sow in tears, in joy shall reap.
7. Those who go forth weeping, bearing their seed,
8. Shall return, on the other hand, in exultation, bringing their sheaves.

(A psalm from Vespers, here without the doxology)

9. Orlando di Lasso: *Epitaphium divi Bernardi: Mira loquor*

Source: Munich, Bayerische Staatsbibliothek, Mus. Ms. 15, f. 60v.

Comments: 45/7/4: precautionary ×.

Translation:

I speak marvellous things, but things worthy of credence.
– Bernard! What is this? Are you still alive?
I am alive.
– You are not dead, then?
By no means.
– And what are you doing?
I am at peace.
– Are you silent or speaking?
Both.
– Why are you silent?
Because I am sleeping.
– Why are you speaking?
Because I am alive.
– What are you speaking?
Holy mysteries.
– To whom?
To the person who reads my writings.
– Surely not to all?
No.
– To whom, then?
Those who seek sweetness.
– Do you have a name?
Yes.
– What?
Bernard, that is a goodly perfume.
– Why perfume?
Because I give off a fragrance.
– What sort of fragrance?
A sweet one.
– For whom do you give off this fragrance and where?
To the reader in the holy book.
– What surname have you?
From the clear valley [of Clairvaux].
– Do you stay there?
I did once, but not now.
– Where do you live now?
On the pinnacle of the mountain.
– What were you like when you lived in the valley?
Humble.
– How important are you now?
I am now as great above, as before I was lowly.
– Does the valley have no part of you?
Yes, it does.
– What?
My bones.
– Until when?
Until the earthly corpse becomes heavenly.

10(a). Orlando di Lasso: *Osculetur me osculo*

Source: Orlando di Lasso, *Fasciculi aliquot sacrarum cantionum cum quatuor, quinque, sex & octo vocibus.* Nuremberg, T. Gerlach, 1582 (RISM L 937): no. 82.

Translation:

O that he would kiss me with the kisses of his mouth! For your fruitfulness is better than wine, the fragrance of your perfume is of the best, like oil poured out is your name: therefore the maidens love you. Draw me after you, let us hurry to the scent of your perfume. The King has brought me into his chambers: we will exult and rejoice in you. We will tell of your fruitfulness more than wine: rightly do they love you.   *(Song of Solomon 1: 2–4)*

10(b). Orlando di Lasso: *Kyrie* (from *Missa super Osculetur me*)

Source: Orlando di Lasso, *Sämtliche Werke, neue Reihe*, vol. 10, ed. S. Hermelink. Kassel & Basel, Bärenreiter, 1970: 187.

Translation:

Lord, have mercy. Christ, have mercy. Lord, have mercy.

(From the Ordinary of the Mass.)

11. Giovanni Pierluigi da Palestrina: *Videntes stellam Magi*

Source: Giovanni Pierluigi da Palestrina, *Le opere complete*, vol. 33, ed. Lino Bianchi. Rome, Istituto Italiano per la Storia della Musica, 1981: 103.

Translation:

When the Magi saw the star, they rejoiced with a great joy, and going into the house they discovered the child with Mary his mother, and prostrating themselves they worshipped him: and opening their treasures they offered him gifts, gold, frankincense, and myrrh.

(Matthew 2: 10–11)

12. Tomás Luis de Victoria: *Magnificat primi toni*

Source: Tomás Luis de Victoria, *Missae, Magnificat, motecta, psalmi, & alia.* Madrid, 'ex typographia regia', 1600 (RISM V 1435): Cantus f. 17r.

Comments: The alternative three-voice canonic setting of v. 5, 'Et misericordia', has been omitted (see *Opera omnia* vol. 3, ed. P. Pedrell, Leipzig 1904/*R*1965, 87). The organ part is notated on four staves with (usually) bar-lines every two breves. In the interests of clarity, strict use has not been made of upward and downward stems, it being easy to check from the vocal staves which part has a particular progression. 107: φ 3 in all parts except B & org. (¢ 3). 115C²(1) & org. 3, 116C²(1)2: precautionary ×. 122: φ3 in all voices. 165: φ 3 in all voices except C² & org. (¢ 3). 181: φ 3 in all voices except A² (φ ½), org. (¢ 3). 217org./1/4: ♩ . 218org./1/2: ♩ . 219org./1/3: ♩ . 220org./1/3: 𐅼 .

Translation:

1. My soul magnifies the Lord.
2. And my spirit has rejoiced in God my saviour.
3. For he has regarded the lowliness of his handmaiden: for behold, from henceforth all generations shall call me blessed.
4. For he who is mighty has magnified me: and holy is his name.

5. And his mercy, throughout all generations, is on those who fear him.
6. He has shown strength with his arm: he has scattered the proud in the imagination of their hearts.
7. He has put down the mighty from their seats, and exalted the humble.
8. The hungry he has filled with good things: and the rich he has sent away empty.
9. He has helped Israel his servant, in remembrance of his mercy.
10. As it was spoken to our forefathers, Abraham and his seed for ever.
11. Glory be to the Father, *etc.*   *(Canticle at Vespers)*

13. Andrea Gabrieli: *Quem vidistis, pastores?*

Source: Concerti di Andrea, et di Gio. Gabrieli organisti. Venice, A. Gardano, 1587 (RISM 1587[(16)]): no. 27.

Comments: 35, 49, 54: signature 3 in all parts.

Translation:
What did you see, shepherds? Tell us, announce to us, who appeared on the earth? A birth we saw, and a chorus of angels praising the Lord. Alleluia.
(Antiphon at Lauds on the Feast of the Nativity)

14. Andrea Gabrieli: *Benedicam Dominum*

Source: Concerti, no. 38.

Translation:
I will bless the Lord at all times: always his praise shall be in my mouth.
In the Lord my soul makes its boast: let the gentle hear and rejoice.
O magnify the Lord with me: and let us exalt his name together.
I sought the Lord diligently, and he heard me: and from all my tribulation he delivered me.
Come near to him, and be radiant: and your faces will not be confounded.
(Ps. 33: 1–5)

15. Giovanni Gabrieli: *O Domine Jesu Christe*

Source: Giovanni Gabrieli, *Opera omnia*, vol. 1, ed. Denis Arnold. Rome, American Institute of Musicology, 1956: 93.

Translation:
O Lord Jesus Christ, wounded on the Cross, drinking gall and vinegar:
I pray to you that your wounding might be the healing of my soul.
(A meditation on the Passion)

16. Giovanni Gabrieli: *Hodie completi sunt*

Source: Giovanni Gabrieli, *Opera omnia*, vol. 3. 1962: 44.

Comments: I have preferred to retain the breve as a bar unit throughout bars 25–35. 21C4, 69C4: accidental as in *Opera omnia*.

Translation:
Today the days of Pentecost are fulfilled, alleluia: today the Holy Spirit appeared in fire to

the disciples, and bestowed on them gifts: he sent them into all the world to proclaim and to testify: that whosoever will believe, and be baptised, will be saved, alleluia.

(Antiphon for the Magnificat at 2nd Vespers of Whit Sunday)

17. Samuel Scheidt: *Nu komm der Heyden Heyland*

Source: Samuel Scheidt, *Werke*, vol. 4, ed. G. Harms. Hamburg, 1933: 56.

Comments: 48/1/1: rest omitted.

Translation:

> Now comes the saviour of the gentiles,
> made known as the child of a virgin,
> of whom all the world will be astonished,
> that God appointed for him such a birth.
> *(Martin Luther, after 'Veni Redemptor gentium', a hymn for Advent)*